Clement Bryce Gunr

Lays of St. Andrews

Clement Bryce Gunn

Lays of St. Andrews

ISBN/EAN: 9783743330283

Manufactured in Europe, USA, Canada, Australia, Japa

Cover: Foto ©ninafisch / pixelio.de

Manufactured and distributed by brebook publishing software
(www.brebook.com)

Clement Bryce Gunn

Lays of St. Andrews

LAYS OF ST. ANDREWS

BY

CLEMENT BRYCE GUNN,

M.D. (EDIN.),

EDITOR OF

"The Three Tales of the Three
Priests of Peebles."

ILLUSTRATED.

ST. ANDREWS : Joseph Cook & Son,
17 and 18 Church Street, and 80 Market Street.

1894.

MATRUM OPTIMÆ
ITINERUM HORUM COMITI
HÆC SOMNIA.

CONTENTS.

I.

Saint Andrews by twilight, from the Pier.

O mystic City of the night!
I view thee through the darkling eve
Which wraps the harbour, where one fain
Would sit and fitful fancies weave.
    O ghostly town!
    O past renown!
    O City of the Martyr's Crown!

Westward a dull gold afterglow
Lights up the Heav'n where set the sun,
And in its radiance low'r the spires
Still standing amid ruin done.
    O fretted glade!
    O pitying shade!
    Concealing havoc wanton made.

B

The glory fills the oriel,
And shines through darkness to the sea;
As anciently at Vespertime
The altar-lights shone cheerfullie.
    O light now spent !
    O Temple rent !
    O service closed when Priestcraft went!

And doth Tintagil mirkly loom,
That castle by the rocky strand,
That with the city seems to sink
Immerged amid the sodden sand?
    O Lyonnesse
    That waves caress !
    O Phantasy of Saintliness !

And thus one sits, and fancy flits
From things to Shades which come and go;
The air is peopled by their Ghosts,
And Priests and Saints pass to and fro.
    But hark that knell !
    Saint Saviour's Bell
    Bids them and me a soft Farewell !

II.

Stations of the Cross.

At Saint Salvator's lychgate hoar,
Within the sound of ocean's roar,
  The Protomartyr Hamilton,
The Cross of pain first bravely bore.

Then Forrest by the Convent Wall
In turn obeyed the Master's call—
  "Take up the Cross and follow Me,"
And cast a beacon-glare o'er all.—

It shone from Fife across the Bay, ╮
Where Angus hills loom faraway,
  And Forfar folks said Malison,
And recked not of the Dawning Day.

And Wishart at the Castle gate,
Where gazed the Cardinal in state,
  In turn the Cross of Suffering bore,
And nobly *tholed* his fateful fate.

And last of all, frail Henry Mill,
Though fourscore years their measure fill,
  Conveyed the Cross the final stage,
And by the Pends fulfilled God's will.

The *Via Dolorosa* trod,
Their souls returned again to God ;
  Their words and testimony live,
And still rolls on the ocean broad !

III.

Saint Mary's Provostry.

Saint Mary's Provostry, Kirkheugh,
  An ancient ruined holy cell,
Whose chants are now the breezes' *sough*,
  Diapasoned with ocean's swell.

Thy ruins stand—a book unsealed,
  And in them lurks a mystery—
Sections of columns half concealed
  Of long-forgotten history.

A Celtic Cross with carven scroll,
  Imbedded lies in masonry ;
The Altar occupies the knoll,
  · Long robbed of sacred blazonry.

A Nave and Chancel unstraight built,
  Intent or error who can tell ? .
And 'gainst them lies the sandy silt
  Of centuries that ages spell.

An Alma Mater is this Fane,
  To that Cathedral proud and high,
Whose turrets rise in cold disdain,
  Unmindful of low ancestry.

For centuries in ages dark,
  Its Altar-light shone o'er the deep,
And cheered the distant fishing-bark,
  Whose toilers work while others
    sleep.

On foreign fleets in war away,
  On embassies in times of peace,
On wrecks half hid 'mid blinding spray,
  Those stones have gazed in scant
    surcease.

And now survives a ruined Nave,
  Dwarf Transepts, and a Chancel bent,
Of Knight and Dame the erstwhile grave,
  Of byegone rites the Monument!

IV.

The Witches' Pool.

See the bairns rush out from School,
Gather at the Witches' Pool!
Work is over, now for play,
'Tis the Witches' drowning day—
Bairns must see the wicked lives
Lived by five decrepit wives,
Suffering the Doom in turn,—
'Witches aye must drown or burn!'
Scriptures plainly counsel give
'Suffer not a Witch to live.'
So the Minister and Kirk
Damning Witches have hot work.
Folks must never rove at night,
Mutter threats nor bairnies fright,
Throw a spell o'er sickly life,
Labour cast on neighbour wife,
Ride a broomstick through the air,
To another's evil swear,
Revels hold on no mirk muir,

Kicking up the Devil's *stour,*
Charges such are those for which
Doited wives are branded WITCH!
Sessions, howe'er *unco guid,*
Ne'er would tell a '*rousing whid,*'
Ne'er a private spite to please
Would condemn old wives like these?
Sternly though their victims try,
Kirks must *live* though Witches *die.*
Proof at times the case may want,
Doubt the mind at others haunt,
Haul the wives then to the Pool,
Test apply by Canon Rule—
Right-hand thumb, to left-hand toe,
Tie—and *vice versa* so.
Now they have them firmly tied,
Like crosses by th' waterside,
Word is given—the tide is full,
Heave all five into the Pool.
Agèd, harmless, lonely wives,
Fastly tied fight for their lives.

Think on't now in later times
Shudder at these legal crimes—
How the guiltless scaled the pyre,
And "possessed" ones 'scaped the fire;
Th' guilt would now be reassessed,
We pronounce the Court "possessed."
Of the wives, some float, some sink,
Pull all five into the brink.
Three exhausted ones are dead,
But o'er them Decree is said—
"They have *sunk* so were good wives."
Can these words bring back their lives?
Wae's me for the other two!
Ah, they *floated* up to view.
Th' true Witch drowns not in the Lake,
Save and burn her at the stake!
Loads of heather, lengths of chain,
Old tar barrels, all are ta'en,
One for each unto the Mound,
Savage multitudes stand round:
Pray'rs are said, of course 'tis fit,

·.   Ask God's Blessing down for it.
Th' piles are fired, the old wives burn,
See the end, then homeward turn.
Smould'ring embers, faggots charred,
Calcined bones, such wives burn hard!
In our ears despairing cries,
Shrieks of dying agonies!
With Mosaic teaching fraught,
What cared we what Jesus taught?

V.
The Tower of Saint Regulus.

Massive windswept ancient Tow'r,
Grimly conscious of thy pow'r,
Standing firm when tempests low'r,
    Saint Regulus.

Relic of an unknown age,
Haply planned by Culdee sage,
Writ upon an unsealed page,
    Saint Regulus.

Abernethy's column stern,
Reared beside the winding Earn,
Kinship claims with thee we learn,
    Saint Regulus.

Cradled in the murky haze,
Shrouding prehistoric ways,
Middle-aged in Romish days,
    Saint Regulus.

When the proud Cathedral reared
Its first turrets—age had seared
Thy grim features—made them weird,
  Saint Regulus.

And throughout the haughty reign,
Lived by the majestic Fane,
Coldly gazed thou in disdain,
  Saint Regulus.

Then when Rome began to pall,
Witnessed thou thy rival's fall,
Standing calm above it all,
  Saint Regulus.

Surged iconoclastic crowd.
Round thy base in fury loud,
To the dust the Abbey bowed,
  Saint Regulus.

Well for thee that taste severe
Graven images kept clear,
Off thy walls unniched and sheer,
  Saint Regulus.

This enabled thee to stand,
Free from harm from raging band,
Saved a monument so grand,
    Saint Regulus.

The Armada timbers gave,—
Rescued from the wrecking wave,
To thy care 'gainst time to save,
    Saint Regulus.

And we scale thy hoary crown,
Scan the academic town,
Thoughtlessly then clamber down,
    Saint Regulus.

And a grim sardonic smile,
Seems to hover o'er the pile,
Seize the day, then—rest awhile,
    Says Regulus.

Men may come and men may go,
Toward the grave they're wending, though
Ages pass—still stand I so,
    Saint Regulus.

VI.

The Terebinth of Tears:

PREACHED BY THE VERY REVD. DR. BOYD,
SEP. 17TH, 1893. GENESIS XXXV., 8.

They bury worn Devòrah,
  Nurse whom a tribe reveres,
Beneath a mighty Oak called
  The Terebinth of Tears.

The wailing stirred the foliage
  Of th' Oak of ancient years,
And christened with their weeping
  The Terebinth of Tears.

In sure anticipation,
  Until the Christ appears,
They leave her in thy keeping,
  O Terebinth of Tears.

Far from thy childhood's country,
· 'Mid scenes of hopes and fears ;
But thou art guarded well by
  Thy Terebinth of Tears.

A Monument of Sorrow,
  In majesty uprears
A leafy crown of verdure,
  The Terebinth of Tears.

The Tree, by far, more ancient
  Than thou, of six score years,
O aged nurse now nursed by
  This Terebinth of Tears.

Of other two handmaidens
  In history one hears:
But grows for Naaman's Captive
  No Terebinth of Tears.

Saint Kieran's Housemaid* slumbers
  From prehistoric years :
Her grave marked by a Boulder ;
  No Terebinth of Tears.

And pilgrims wander thither,
  Each maid her worth reveres
'Mid Irish scenes ; though shades it
  No Terebinth of Tears.

Thus Housemaid, Nurse, and Captive,
    Of old or tender years,
May earn undying mem'ry
    Their Terebinth of Tears.

---

* " On our way to the Nunnery (Devorguilla's, near
the Shannon), we noticed a large stone apparently
cut for a Font at the place which, in Dr. Healy's
plan, is marked by the quaint title 'Grave of St.
Kierau's Housemaid.'" — *A Pilgrimage on the
Anniversary of Saint Kieran, Sep. 8, 1893.*

VII.

The Cemetery, Saint Andrews.

God's Rood within the Convent wall,
　Encircled by the sounding sea,
A blest abode of sunlit peace;
　A smiling land it seems to me.

No dread of death its beauty haunts,
　No spectral phantom of the grave ;
But God's own glory lights the Garth,
　And gilds the wrecked Cathedral Nave.

The peace of God broods o'er the scene,
　Broke only by the murm'ring sea ;
In drowsy monotone that breaks
　But mars not Heaven's harmony.

Wellnigh in love with 'easeful death';
　This sacred soil enamours one
To yield the fevered fretful life,
　And slumber here when all is done.
C

Beneath the ruined Abbey Wall
   In company with saintly men,
One's dust might rest—the Spirit flit,
   And visit this sweet scene again.

And in the gloaming dusk, the note
   Of sweet Saint Saviour's bell would peal,
And permeate with melody,
   And o'er the spirit softly steal.

God's acre this in very truth,
   The pride of intellect lies here ;
The learned, the good, the brave, the strong,
   Without reproach, withouten fear.

And yet methinks the heart is touched,
   By one lone spot of strangers' graves,
Where rest at last the sailors done
   To death, amid the raging waves.

But not to-day are storm-tossed seas,
   The ocean smiles blue and serene,
And gently laps the rocky coast,
   And sparkles in the sunny sheen.

And stern Saint Regulus stands grim
    Amid the fastly filling sward ;
·Men come, men go, the ages roll,   ·
    His tower o'er all keeps watch and ward.

VIII.

Alone upon Saint Regulus Tower.

Around me on the bartizan God's living
 Presence lies,
His Æther breathing life and love diffus-
 ing to the skies ;
And at one's feet the Academic City
 westward trends,
Each ancient street convergingly to the
 Cathedral wends—
The apex of the city life—all paths lead
 to the Grave—
Hard bye the ruined pillared arcades of
 the roofless nave.
Afar, the azure ocean scintillates in
 morning light
And rumbling murmurs from its waters
 vibrate in the height ;
And through the murmur run the chimes
 from many a city spire,
Each gleaming through the seaborn haze
 like pinnacles of fire.

At once in circling sweep, with voice
    untuned, wild seafowl sped,
Like tortured spirits blindly flying rising
    from the dead ;
But through their cry a burst of song
    wafts on the fitful breeze,
Ascending from the Priory Choir lodged
    amid the trees;
Then on the seafowl whirled and vanished
    on their devious ways,
While still uprose the warbled hymn—a
    melody of praise.
And thus methought 'tis so with man,
    misfortunes may come fleet,
Yet fleetly pass and leave to rise God's
    music full and sweet.
Alone with God I hold this tower and
    gaze upon the earth,
One's worries vanish, hope revives, ideals
    have their birth,
Would that they lived to fructify, alas for
    man is weak,

Our heavenly glimpses weaker grow as
earth one's footsteps seek.
But still these meditative moments serve
to feed the fire,
Of love divine which glows in each and
force one to aspire.

IX.

Quaedam Umbrae, St. Andrews.

A city of deep mystery,
  This Classic town of Academic lore,
Which Souls who once made history
  As Shades pervade though clothed in
    flesh no more.

Their Presence fills the atmosphere,
  When night benignant mother darkles
    deep,
And no sound stirreth save the moan
  Of melancholy waves which never sleep.

And Belfries Aëreal pour
  Soft hourly chimes upon the list'ning
    night ;
'Tis then the ghostly Shadows throng,
  Assuming phantom outlines to the sight.

Faint strains of heavenly music swell,
  A glimm'ring flicker lights the mid-
    night hour,

And shows a Form in shadow wrapt ;
   Saint Regulus is hov'ring o'er his tower.

Dim will-o-wisps light up the nave,
   Whose ruined walls rise gaunt against
      the sky,
And in their feeble sparks one sees
   A crowd of Ghosts stripped of mortality.

Churchmen and Laymen jostle close,
   As fleeting clouds upon an autumn
      breeze ;
And many a Form of high degree
   And low, are what the awestruck gazer
      sees.

The Martyred and the Slayers here
   Are mingled, and have long since
      found the right ;
And some who struck and some who
   tholed,
   Their small selves view in the Eternal
      Sight.

And Betoun, the proud Cardinal,
  With Norman Leslie's Shadow standing
      by,
In dread no longer, for is sealed
  · The doom of every mortal as they die.

And One—far-seeing in his age,
  Who guided Scotland in her darksome
      day,
And founded Saint Salvator's, strode
  With   golden   mace—good   Bishop
      Kennedy.

The Shades of Prelates muster well
  Their ghostly phantom Hierarchy
      round,
And all the names in history,
  With scores unnoted, here as Shades
      are found.

And Sharpe, first Presbyter, then Priest,
  In blood-stained cassock shuffles dimly
      by ;
Two Churches showed him how to live,
  And yet the murdered prelate had to die.

And Chastelar perfervid soul,
  The luckless lover of a lovely Queen,
A headless Shade pervades the night
  Alone in grim and solitary mien.

And clanking chains a group reveal,
  George Wishart, Forrest, saintly
      Hamilton,
And Henry Mill—the old and last
To burn as martyrs 'mid priests' malison.

And in the witches' neuk old dames,
  The tortured martyrs of Kirk Session
      Rule,
Sit cow'ring, chatt'ring by themselves,
  In bitter memory of former dule.

But night advances, and the *sough*
  Of rising breezes tells of coming dawn ;
Light streams in pencils from the east,
  And all the ghostly Shades have ghostly
      gone!

X.

The Last Saint.

There stands upon the Abbey Wall
    Without restraint,
Sole relic of its statues all—
    A broken Saint!

A stone Madonna and the Child,
    In mute complaint,
Wrecked remnant of the shrines defiled—
    A lonely Saint!

Why spared the mob this statue lone?
    Did rage grow faint?
And late repentance pity own,
    For one poor Saint?

Or haply the Iconoclast,
    With reason quaint,
Spared her as symbol of the past—
    A sample Saint!

And now the Virgin holds the gate,
  In stony plaint!
A vain appealing against fate—
  From one last Saint!

Nor need we for a ritual dead,
  Of grief make feint,
The time was full, the day had sped—
  For Priest and Saint!

But later days will hail a creed
  Withouten taint ;
Eternal truth from error freed—
  Replace the Saint.

XI.

A Summer Sea—From the Castle.

The scintillating silent sea
Here stilly slumbers in the sun,
Encurtained by a misty haze,
And hushed its deep diapason.

The faintest streak of lightest foam,
A tiny ripple on the shore,
Alone betoken slumb'ring force,
The whisper of a giant's roar.

The wavelets roll the fragile shells;—
Intact sea urchins up the sand,
But those same waters wrecked brave
    barks,
Whose ribs loom gauntly on the strand.

The offing lowers hazily
Around the circle of the sea,
And veils from curious scrutiny
A depth of secret mystery.

Perchance then this the reason why
Beyond the grave no sea exist,
Its secrets, partings, depths, and storms,
With boundless bliss may not consist.

And by these Colleges and Towers,
And ruins of a mighty past,
Its waves have rolled for aeons long,
And roll they will while time shall last.

Then muse no more upon a theme
Whose ancientness scorns vain essay;
No voice can tell its mighty spell,
Its poesy and mystery.

From Photograph by]

Valentine & Son, Dublin.

RUINS OF CATHEDRAL.

XII.

The Passing of the Principal.

The Very Rev Principal Cunningham, D.D.
buried Sep. 6, 1893.

Under the Limes 'mid sonorous chimes,
 That sadden the afternoon ;
With mournful tone 'neath leaves russet
  grown,
 That fall to the breezes' *croon.*

With measured beat up the ancient street,
 Furth of the College they go;
And leaves rustling fall on the funeral
  pall,
 Whispering gently and slow.

They bear to his grave, past the ruined
  nave,
 The aged and worn Principal,
A Schoolman of thought from the School
  where he taught,
 To his grave by the convent wall.

And there within sound of sea and in
    ground
  Holy and peacefully fair,
Ashes and earth to their kind in the Garth
  They leave to commingle there.

Safe *happed* 'neath the sod, and the soul
    to God
  Has returned and truth discerned ;
How vain are the Schools, and the wisest
    fools,
  In light of verity learned.

And the Scarlet Gown has marched back
    to town,
  And Presbyter gone—and Priest,
And noble by birth[1] and noble of earth[2]
  Have left their chief to his rest.

And the grey old stones in their
    monotones,
  Look dim now the robes have gone,
That varied the view in diversified hue,
  'Gainst tombs on the grassy lawn.

So the pageant hath passed that cometh
    at last,
  Though humbler to you and me ;
But that sad band had environment
    grand,
  In the city by the sea.

---

1. The Most Noble the Marquess of BUTE,
    Lord Rector.
2. Very Rev. Principal CAIRD, D.D.

D

XIII.

The Stone Christ on St. Salvators.

Saint Saviour's Tow'r looks on the town,
  Saint Saviour's Face upon the street ;
A Christ of stone, placed high alone
  Above the tread of hurrying feet.
And thus for ages has Christ watched,
  Amid the rush and change of time,
With th' steady gaze of ancient days,
  'Mid storms that vex the northern clime.

The tender lad from boyhood's home,
  With the home-glint still in his eye,
As he donned th' gown and marched
    adown
  The Northgait in new dignity,
A passing glance might cast on Thee
  And heedless hurry through the Pend ;
He crossed the porch—passed on the
    torch,
  He passed in turn—Thou saw'st the
    end.

Argyle, Montrose, and men whose lives
  Lay hidden in the scroll of fate ;
Men of the hour, when perils low'r,
  Have passed Thee by the ancient gate.
And One upheld the might of Rome,
  Another came and smashed her keys,
And th' Elder grim succeeded him,
  And all the time Thou studied these.

For all swore by the name of Christ,
  And in His name the others burned
Priest, and Witch, and Heretic—such
  As dogmas of the others spurned.
And centuries rolled swiftly on,
  And rampant ruin raged throughout ;
But 'mid the strife, the truth had life,
  And flickered feebly—well nigh out.

And so the Christ survived the wreck
  Of Abbey and Cathedral grand ;

·   An Augur good that never should
     The truth pass wholly from the land.
So on Saint Saviour's Church still stands
     The Saviour from His niche unhurled
What change betides, He still abides,
     The Saviour of a fallen world.

XIV.

The Well Deserted.

Abandoned is the Holy Well,
  Gone all the devotees,
Who erstwhile crowded round its font
  To seek health in disease.

Soul-heal, as well as body-cure,
  Its Holy Waters wrought ;
Indulgence too, for favoured sin,
  Might e'en at times be bought.

A plan of high convenience this
  From sin the *soul* to shrive,
Then quaff in faith the holy draught,
  And cause the *body* thrive.

Then with Indulgence in the pouch
  The homeward way begin,
And well absolved for all the past,
  Resume the dear loved sin.

No saintly name adorns the font,
    It stands—a god unknown—
Amid the tombs, itself a tomb,
    Unworshipped and alone!

The grave of superstition deep,
    The end of long-nursed hope,
When faith unbounded failed to cure,
    And left the mind to grope—

In spiritual darkness deep,
    And hopeless as of Hell;
Till dawned the light, and as of old,
    Truth lurked within a well!

" Drinkers of Saint Leonard's Well,"
    The Priests the New School term,
Unconscious that *their* well is doomed
    And truth has sprung its germ.

And now a muddy pool stagnates
    Where limped waters flowed,
A shrine abandoned—virtue lost—
    A darksome dank abode.

Round it shines Heaven's glorious light,
   Its pencils kiss the green ;
The Well is but a relic now
   Of systems that have been.

XV.

The Bottle Dungeon.

Forth of the Bottle Dungeon
    The immured Shadows go,
As the Geni of the Arabian Tale
    From his Bottle long ago.

Upon the mirk mirk midnight
    The trooping columns pour,
And their gathering march is the mono-
        tone
    Of the surf upon the shore.

Far down below th' Castle wall
    The waves break now, as then,
When the Shadows inhabited flesh and
        blood
    In that dark and loathsome den.

When Wishart lay 'mid darkness
    But Light within Heav'nsent,
He bravely administered forth of that hell
    The Protestant Sacrament.

ST ANDREWS CASTLE

From Photograph by]

[Valentine & Son, Dundee

And later there lay th' body
  Of th' slaughtered Cardinal.
"All is lost"! on his lips as th' spirit
    escaped
  From the burdened body's thrall.

And many nameless pris'ners
  Within it ebbed out life
By hunger's dread pangs, or more merci-
    ful rope,
  Or the hired assassin's knife.

Whose hell-born mind designed it,
  And who the rock explored,
And who was the judge who a fellowman
    bade
  Into its depths be lowered ?

Alack! that Cave holds secrets
  Vast as the ocean deep :
The sickness of hope deferred, ravings
    and shrieks,
  And th' tears that pris'ners weep.

And above, God's sunlight smiles,
  The earth lies fair around,
And the summer seas sing the low
      lullabies
  Of the wretches underground.

Providence spells mystery :
  Inscrutable His ways;
Though a purpose Divine lurked amid
      the depths
  Of this Cave of ancient days.

Thank God we live in the light.
  I dream, but while I sit,
Their spirits excarnate have gone to their
      rest ;
  'Twas fancy that made them flit.

And this darksome hole remains
  A show for aged carles
Which they prate all about to an awe-
      struck crowd,
  And then ?   They pocket their arles !

XVI.

The Hospice of Saint Regulus.

A Garden of fair women is Saint Rule's,—
A posy of the choicest from the Schools
Which Academic titles maidens give,
And here these Damosels of learning live
Who form the Sources of Saint Leonard's
  Well,
Whence maidens drink in knowledge, and
  excel
In all that makes sound body and sound
  mind,
Nor spurn the Course's cope—a Soul
  refined.
Here then the Mistresses reside, and they
Live 'neath their Prioress's gentle sway,
And many maids of *high degree* dwell
  here—
The Wrangler of her College and her
  year.

The B.A., B.Sc., and L.L.A.
Of old Saint Andrews, *titled dames* are
    they.
And Creeds of diverse Churches too
    abound,
And maids who own but small beliefs are
    found
Within this charmed Retreat—a Nun's
    abode,
For all who seek by straight or devious
    road
Eternal Truth.   These Vestals keep
    alight
The Sacred Fire, and hand their torches
    bright
On down the years.   And Happiness
    dwells here,
Because their lives are full from year to
    year—
A harmony of chords—a tuneful School,
Where Life and Home and Thought are
    beautiful.

I muse upon this Hospice and its Head,
The brown-eyed gentle ladye who hath
    fled,
The Border and the Country Manse to be
Head of this Women's Hospice by the
    sea,
And from her windows, southward to the
    Braes,
I see again the golden yellow haze
That broods upon the bending Autumn
    corn
And promises a beauteous Harvest morn.
And through the vision peal the Sunday
    bells
That jangle on the air, ev'n to the cells,
Where each Recluse her private study
    holds,
And to her special taste its features
    moulds:
—The High Church devotee, a crucifix,
Or sketch ecclesiastic will affix
On wall. Diana's Votaress o'erhead
A hunting-crop and iron shoe instead :

The Wrangler, Gallio-like, doth not care
For trifles such, so leaves her walls all
    bare.
The maid aesthetic, with a well-lined
    purse,
Adorns her cell in Art, good, bad, or
    worse.
And thus these rooms their tenants in-
    dicate
As pious, learnèd, cultured, or sedate.
But every maiden feels that home is here
With love and comfort and the best of
    cheer,
And happiness throughout, because con-
    tent,
And thus in busy usefulness the golden
    hours are spent.

XVII.

On the Tower—An Autumn Eve.

I stood on the Tow'r and pondered,
  While ocean sang below,
And the winds were sweeping by me,
  And I watched th' waters flow.

And round me the leaves were falling
  Consumed by th' Autumn Fire
And their dirge the wind was wailing
  On th' chords of Nature's Lyre.

And the heart within grew sadder
  As I saw th' Summer die ;
Perchance then too one remembered
  Old friends who lifeless lie.

Death's mystery, who can fathom,
  Or who hath th' secret read ;
The Bowl is broke, and loosed the Cord,
  Th' animate Form lies dead.

Oh, hard 'tis to die in Summer,
   When th' fields are all aglow
With living sheen and lovely green
   That naught of fading know.

And the radiant sunsets leading
   Th' thoughts to another land,
That seems to bound th' Horizon's edge,
   Outside of th' golden band.

And oh, if a Land there lieth
   Of th' lovely and the brave,
Mayhap a man might yield this life
   And enter th' darksome grave.

But winds must howl and dead leaves fall,
   And beauty lifeless lie,
Ere hope grows cold and life grows old,
   And I lie down to die!

XVIII.

The Lade Braes—Autumn.

Alas for the happy harvest fields
  And the pleasure now gone for aye,
And the friends of yore now seen no more
  On the bonnie bright Summer day;
And the laughing breeze swept through
      the trees,
  And the corn heaps kissed as it went,
Then on careered and the weary cheered
  With the fragrance the fields had lent.

And merrily trickled th' silver burn,
  And how gaily the long corn waved,
And the gentle beams in glowing streams
  With gold liquid the full ears laved ;
And the winds still sweep and dews still
      weep
For the death of the Autumn day,
While weary and worn alone I mourn
  For the old time now gone away.

E

And still they bury the golden seed
  And then reap it in golden grain,
But the wild oats sown are quickly grown
  And yield but wild harvest again;
And many one sighs and broken dies
  For the chances of youth long lost
And seedtime gone; but mem'ry alone
  Aye reminds of the bitter cost.

XIX.

Divine Service in the Town Church.

We entered Holy Trinity,
                    Doctor Boyd,
And hearked to thy Divinity,
                    Overjoyed ;
For here was no Service bald
Nor a preacher dry and *cauld*,
But Priest and Presbyter in one,
                    Doctor Boyd.

And the Service had a Ritual,
                    Doctor Boyd,
And potency Spiritual
                    Unalloyed ;
And we readily "responsed"
From our corner snug esconsed,
And thus did *our own* devotions,
                    Doctor Boyd.

But a dread of innovation,
           Doctor Boyd,
Which imperils their salvation,
           And is void
Haunts the timid minds of some,
So to matins will not come,
Dreading lest they thus encourage
           Doctor Boyd.

But *these* follow paths divisive,
           Doctor Boyd,
For the Scriptures are decisive,
           And thee buoyed ;
For the Bible somewhere says
" Stand ye in the ancient ways,"
This you have essayed to do,
           Doctor Boyd.

The Innovators are the Folk,
           Doctor Boyd,
Who in service never spoke,
           And annoyed

Folks such actually feel,
As the anthems o'er them steal,
·Quite forgetting that's the *old* way,
          Doctor Boyd.

Their ways have lasted over long,
          Doctor Boyd,
We want a fuller praise of Song,
          Well employed
In praising God divinely,
Not weakly and supinely,
Giving Him the best and sweetest,
          Doctor Boyd.

We need no more a " praying-wheel,"
          Doctor Boyd,
But with a Book of Prayer to kneel,
          And we " joyed
When to the House of God they said
Go up," and have God's Blessing shed
On a Service chaste and holy,
          Doctor Boyd.

XX.

The last Walk---Sunday Evening.

Mere words alone can never tell,
　　Nor art of painter fancy please,
To sing or paint the magic spell,
　　The glory of these Autumn Seas.

That farewell walk, could we forego?
　　Around the Convent Wall at eve,
We sauntered in the afterglow
　　That gave the night a brief reprieve.

The stilly twilight lay around,
　　Above gleamed bright the turret light,
The gentle breeze conveyed the sound
　　Of tiny ripples hid from sight.

Within the Cloister-garth lies still
　　The peopled city of the dead,
Cleric and Layman, good and ill,
　　At peace within their sea-girt bed.

And round the Walls and by the Quay
  We musing strolled ; and on the Pier
We sat and listened to the sea,
  And sought its message deep to hear.

The City lurked in ghostly shade,
  Begemmed with many a twinkling light,
Its spires and tow'rs and crowsteps fade
  Even as we gaze and all is night !

And passing Kirkheugh's ruined walls
  We skirt the spot where Forrest burned,
The stars peep forth as darkness falls
  Upon our way now homeward turned.

The moated Keep looms eerily,
  Saint Saviour tolls the curfew low,
We wake from fancy cheerilie,
  Again into the glare we go.

www.ingramcontent.com/pod-product-compliance
Lightning Source LLC
Chambersburg PA
CBHW032043090426
42733CB00030B/639